Tick Tock and

Written by Fiona Undrill

Illustrated by Jon Stuart

Collins

Tick Tock is sick.

Mick is not sick.

Tick Tock did nap.

Mick did not nap.

Tick Tock is sad.

Mick is not sad.

Tick Tock can kick.

Mick can not kick.

Tick Tock is on top.

Mick is not on top.

Tick Tock is in.

Mick is not in.

14

15

🐾 Review: After reading 🐾

Use your assessment from hearing the children read to choose any GPCs, words or tricky words that need additional practice.

Read 1: Decoding

- Ask the children to sound talk and blend each of the following words: s/i/ck, k/i/ck, c/a/n.
- Can the children think of any words that rhyme with **Tock**? (e.g. *sock, lock, frock, block, rock*)
- Look at the "I spy sounds" pages (14–15). Discuss the picture with the children. Can they find items/examples of words that contain the /c/ and "ck" sounds? (*duck, sock, bucket, crocodile, cat, cap, cloud, catch*)

Read 2: Prosody

- Model reading each page with expression to the children.
- After you have read each page, ask the children to have a go at reading with expression.
- Encourage children to have fun practising reading the words **Tick Tock** with expression, like a clock ticking, using different voices and tones.
- Show the children how to use expression and tone to emphasise the opposites in the book.

Read 3: Comprehension

- For every question ask the children how they know the answer. Ask:
  - Who was feeling sick? (*Tick Tock*)
  - Why could Mick not kick a ball? (*he didn't have his football boots*)
  - Look at page 13. What is Mick doing outside? (*playing on his scooter*)
  - What activities do you like to do outside? (e.g. *ride a bike, football, tennis, playing with friends*)
  - This book is about opposites. Can you think of any opposites? (e.g. *high/low, up/down, clean/dirty, big/small*)